Believe in Love

A SIDDHA YOGA® PUBLICATION
PUBLISHED BY SYDA FOUNDATION
www.siddhayoga.org

Published by SYDA Foundation
371 Brickman Rd, PO Box 600,
South Fallsburg, New York 12779, USA

Acknowledgments

Design: Cheryl Crawford
Cover Illustration: Shane Conroy
Editors: Susan Baker, Peggy Bendet, Valerie Sensabaugh

Printed in the United States of America
First published 2000

05 04 03 02 01 00   5 4 3 2 1

Library of Congress Catalog Card Number 00-131171
ISBN 0-911307-86-9

Copyright acknowledgments appear on pages 58-61
Printed on recycled paper

Contents

Believe in Love

Foreword

*F*rom the most ancient of times, teachers in the various religious traditions of the world have instructed spiritual seekers to practice a special kind of contemplation in which aspirants read or listen attentively to concise passages of scripture or to powerful words of sages. Seekers then quietly and with deep reverence reflect on the inner significance of the teachings and search within themselves for ways to apply those lessons in their own lives.

In Christian monasticism, for example, monks and nuns who yearn for a taste of God's presence practice what is known as *lectio divina*, holy reading, in which they prayerfully meditate on short passages from scripture as a way to gain inspiration and deeper wisdom. Tradition regards the imbibing of sacred truths in this way as nourishment of the soul and in fact quite vividly describes the process as *ruminatio*, literally a slow and repeated chewing of the sacred words that leads to the release of their full flavor.

In India, such rumination on a sacred text or lesson from one's spiritual teacher may be said to lead to the tasting of *rasa*, the ambrosial essence of the sublime. According to Abhinavagupta, the great Kashmiri Siddha of the eleventh century, *rasāsvāda* is similar to *brahmāsvāda:* the taste of such an essence is comparable to the taste of the Divine itself.

But virtually all religious traditions in India hold that such a nectarean flavor cannot be tasted without diligent and attentive spiritual discipline. Such discipline necessarily includes a number of different yet related practices, one of the most honored of which has always been that of *svādhyāya*, a term we may translate as "self-reflection" or "recitation by oneself." Undertaking *svādhyāya*, a spiritual seeker quietly chants mantras, recites *sūtras*, sings sacred *gītās*, studies texts, or repeats words spoken by the Guru. While doing so, he or she inwardly contemplates their deeper meaning.

The *Bhagavad Gītā* reports Krishna's teaching to Arjuna that *svādhyāya* is one of the divine virtues. In the second century B.C.E., the great sage Patanjali saw *svādhyāya* to be so important that he listed it among five primary yogic disciplines without which there can be no true spiritual growth. (The other four are moral and physical purity, the cultivation of inner contentment or equanimity, fervent dedication to one's practice, and devotion to God.)

Patanjali taught that *svādhyāya* joins with fervent practice and devotion to God to form what he called the "yoga of action" and that the study of sacred words is such an effective practice that it leads to communion with the Divine. In roughly the eighth century, the teacher Vedavyasa similarly asserted that "the gods, the visionary seers, and the Siddhas themselves become visible to one who practices *svādhyāya*."

But the spiritual traditions of India also hold that, having heard or read a powerful teaching, a seeker must endeavor to bring the liberating insights and transformative truths presented by those words into effect in his or her life. Otherwise the words merely entertain, mystify, or even clutter the mind. The Siddhas teach us that true contemplation is part of a process: hearing, contemplating, understanding, imbibing, and becoming. As Swami Muktananda has said, "Knowledge that is not put into action is a burden."

The contemplations in this book are tools to help you in your own version of *svādhyāya*. You may wish to focus on one particular passage for a period of time. Memorize it, perhaps, or write it down so that you can carry it with you wherever you go. Record your thoughts inspired by the wisdom reflected in these teachings; you will surely delight in the bright gems you thus have mined from the quiet integrity of your own soul.

This collection is part of a series, each book of which contains a set of contemplations centered on a different aspect of the spiritual life. These contemplations are not merely pleasant or interesting thoughts; they are selections from scriptures as well as lessons from philosophers and teachings from ancient and modern saints. They possess *shabda-vīrya*, the "potency of sacred words," the power of which can transform your life and strengthen your spiritual discipline.

Contemplating them, we somehow inwardly recognize the Truth these words outwardly express. This is because the same Truth lies within each of us. It may be that much of the time that Truth is, for us, still vague and unformed because we have not found the words with which to express it. These contemplations give us those words. Reflecting on them can therefore inspire the awakening and blossoming of our own inner wisdom.

Ruminate slowly on these teachings. Relish their delectable essence. Let them nourish you.

William K. Mahony
Department of Religion
Davidson College
Davidson, North Carolina

Introduction

*I*s there anything more transforming, compelling, fulfilling, re-
deeming, and yet more ineffable than
genuine love? In a talk on her New
Year's message for 2000, "Believe in
Love," Gurumayi Chidvilasananda
quotes a classical Indian text on
devotion, *Narada's Bhakti Sūtras:* "The
nature of love cannot be defined."
Even so, as she says, there is no
topic more worthy of contemplation
than love.

What does it mean to believe in

love? It may be that our own associations with the word *love* carry us into the realm of romance or family, vocation or heritage, or any number of the dimensions of life we find meaningful. The passages in this little book encompass them all. According to the saints and sages quoted herein, love is the divine foundation on which all life rests.

The great devotional scriptures of India teach us that to cultivate and purify our experience of love is a sadhana, a genuine spiritual path. On this path, the means is love and the goal is, again, love. The goal is supreme love, *parābhakti*, which is a total identification with the unconditional love that is both God's nature and the essence of our own awakened souls.

The sadhana of love is not always easy. We may wish to live in our hearts but find that we get distracted from this great intention. The main obstacle on the path of love is our own ego, whose pernicious self-centered motivations, desires, and demands distort and obscure our love for others and for God. To believe in love we need to turn away from the constricting path of self-concern. Thus, drawing once again on *Narada's Bhakti Sūtras*, Gurumayi says that the way to overcome the ego is "by uninterrupted loving service."

Just a few short words offer such profound guidance! Through service we come to know the love that is God's nature, and we can offer this service in even the most immediate circumstances of our lives. It is this day-by-day, moment-by-moment offering of service that expands our experience of love. In her talk, Gurumayi stresses the value of drawing on the great virtues such as kindness, goodwill, compassion, courtesy, and respect for others as a means of making love more visible.

This is guidance for leading a fulfilled life. In a simple and mysterious way, the very goal of spiritual work, our merging with God, is impelled through everyday acts of appreciation and consideration for others. We may ask, as does Hafiz, "What is the door to God?" And, like that Sufi sage, we can know that this doorway is "in the face of everyone I see."

The concise passages in this little book give us much to ruminate on regarding the nature of love, the ego as the obstacle to love, the importance of cultivating the virtues, and the experience of the holy presence that comes when we truly open into love. May Gurumayi's message

"Believe in Love" take root deep in our being, and may our contemplation of this noble theme be of help to us as we move along the path of love.

— WKM

Believe in Love

Love is yoga, love is knowledge, love is peace, love is medicine, love is wealth; love is the greatest treasure of the heart. Love is the magnet that attracts the divine power. Therefore, love and let love flow in your heart.

SWAMI MUKTANANDA

As great and transforming as love is, it is also very mysterious. To make an attempt to define love can be as foolish as trying to build a bridge from the earth to the sky. Nonetheless, it is even more foolish not to try and understand love.

GURUMAYI CHIDVILASANANDA

There is a love like a small lamp that goes out when the oil is consumed, or like a stream that dries up when it doesn't rain. But there is a love that is like a mighty spring gushing up out of the earth; it keeps flowing forever, and is inexhaustible.

ISAAC OF NINEVEH

The life-giving treasure
Lies hidden in your own heart.
Do not seek it from street to street
And from door to door.

SWAMI RAMA TIRTHA

The heart is the hub of all
sacred places.
Go there and roam.

BHAGAWAN NITYANANDA

*G*reat is the overflow of Divine Love, which is never still but ever ceaselessly and tirelessly pours forth, so that our little vessel is filled to the brim and overflows. If we do not choke the channel with self-will, God's gifts continue to flow and overflow.

MECHTHILD OF MAGDEBURG

The Beloved looked at me and said,

How can you go on living
without me?

I said,

I swear, like a fish out of water.

He said,

Then why do you hold so tight
to the dry land?

JALAL AL-DIN RUMI

The cup of the heart
Is overflowing with wine,
So why this thirst for joy in objects?
Break the seal of the ego
And drink the wine of divinity.

SWAMI RAMA TIRTHA

Go sweep out the chamber
of your heart.
Make it ready to be
the dwelling place
of the Beloved.
When you depart out,
He will enter it.
In you, void of yourself,
will He display His beauties.

MAHMUD SHABISTARI

When you get closer to ego, you get far from others; when you get far from ego, you get closer to others and you also get closer to God.
Talk to your ego like this:

What are you so proud of?
All you have done for me is to
alienate me from God, from wisdom,
from humanity. So what is there
for you to get inflated about?

The ego hasn't done anything good.... It has dried up the heart, making it sterile—the heart where love should have been throbbing all the time.

SWAMI MUKTANANDA

*L*et loving lead your soul.
Make it a place to retire to,
a kind of monastery cave, a retreat
for the deepest core of being.

Then build a road
from there to God.

FARID AL-DIN ATTAR

Listen, my dear ones. Begin the change with *Narada's Bhakti Sūtras:* "By uninterrupted loving service." Start by glorifying God, by appreciating your life, by admiring others and sharing good things with others, by planting the beneficial seeds of the virtues as you go through your day, by checking your emotions and making sure before you say or do something that it will benefit others, and by being brave enough to allow the ego to transform.

GURUMAYI CHIDVILASANANDA

O thou dweller in my heart,
open it out, purify it,
    make it bright and beautiful,
awaken it, prepare it, make it fearless,
make it a blessing to others,
rid it of laziness, free it from doubt,
unite it with all, destroy its bondage,
let thy peaceful music
    pervade all its works.
Make my heart fixed
    on thy holy lotus feet
and make it full of joy, full of joy,
    full of joy.

PRAYER SUNG IN MAHATMA GANDHI'S
SATYAGRAHA ASHRAM

The best portion of a good man's life
is his little, nameless, unremembered
acts of kindness and love.

WILLIAM WORDSWORTH

Make many acts of love,
for they set the soul on fire
and make it gentle.

TERESA OF AVILA

Hari is like sugar spilled in the sand
that an elephant cannot pick up —
Says Kabir, the Guru gave me the hint:
Become an ant and eat it!

KABIR

*P*eople mistakenly think that sadhana, the spiritual journey, either makes you feel so intoxicated that you lose touch with reality or it is so severe and tormenting that you perish. Sadhana is neither of these. It is your connection with your own Self. Learn to have regard for the sadhana process: the inner purification, the blossoming of the inner Self, the nectarean fruit, the blazing fire.

GURUMAYI CHIDVILASANANDA

What you think is you
is exactly what covers you.
If this cloud gets wiped from your sight,
you'll be gone —
Only the Beloved will remain.
Then an inner voice will say:

That eternal light, which you have veiled,
rises like the dawn —
That truth, forever concealed,
is at last made known:
You are the veil,
You are the Beloved,
You carry yourself
in your own Secret Heart.

FAKHRUDDIN ARAQI

During our work and other activities, we should stop as often as we can, for a moment, to adore God from the bottom of our hearts, to savor Him, by stealth as it were, as He passes by. Since you know God is with you in all your actions, that He is in the deepest recesses of your soul, why not, from time to time, leave off your external activities and even your spoken prayers to adore Him inwardly, to praise Him, to petition Him, to offer Him your heart, and to give Him thanks?

BROTHER LAWRENCE

The important thing is to love much, and so do that which best stirs you to love. It doesn't consist in great delight but in desiring with strong determination to please God in everything.

TERESA OF AVILA

Here love, O here love . . .
with your heart on duty
To the souls of rivers,
children, forest animals,
All the shy feathered
ones and laughing, jumping,
Shining fish.
O here, pilgrim,
Love
On this holy battleground of life.

HAFIZ

The true man of God sits in the midst of his fellow-men, and rises and eats and sleeps and marries and buys and sells and gives and takes in the bazaars and spends the days with other people, and yet never forgets God even for a single moment.

ABU SA'ID IBN ABI'L-KHAYR

What is important is to look upon everyone with a deep sense of honor, because your own heart and mind are influenced by the way you look at others. If we could do just that, we would be rendering the greatest service to our fellow beings; and the reward of that service would be inner peace and God-realization.

SWAMI MUKTANANDA

You never enjoy the world aright . . . till you love men so as to desire their happiness with a thirst equal to the zeal of your own; till you delight in God for being good to all; you never enjoy the world.

THOMAS TRAHERNE

Question: We are commanded to love our neighbor as ourself. But if I see a man who is wicked before God, how can I love him?

Rabbi Shmelke: Love your neighbor like something which you yourself are. For all souls are one. Don't you know that the original soul came out of the essence of God, and that every human soul is a part of God? And will you have no mercy on Him, when you see that one of His holy sparks has been lost in a maze, and is almost stifled?

*K*now him to be a true human being
Who takes to his bosom
those who are in distress.
Know that God resides in the heart
of such a one.
His heart is saturated with gentleness
through and through.

TUKARAM MAHARAJ

Verily, so long as we enjoy
the light of day,
May we greet each other
with love.
Verily, so long as we enjoy
the light of day,
May we pray for one another.

ZUNI PRAYER

$\mathcal{L}$et the good in me connect with the good in others, until all the world is transformed through the compelling power of love.

RABBI NACHMAN

Remember nothing is small in the eyes of God. Do all that you do with love.

THERESE OF LISIEUX

Question: Please explain perfect virtue.

Confucius: It is, when you go abroad, to behave to everyone as if you were receiving a great guest; to employ the people as if you were assisting at a great sacrifice; not to do to others as you would not wish done to yourself.

The virtues such as kindness and friendliness hold love. Gentleness and tenderness offer love. Generosity and altruism sustain love. Goodwill and benevolence deliver love. Compassion and empathy embody love. Simple things like courtesy and respect convey love. When love manifests through these pathways, it stirs every heart with the power of love. You perceive the face of love on this earth.

GURUMAYI CHIDVILASANANDA

I have just three things to teach:
simplicity, patience, compassion.
These three are your greatest treasures.
Simple in actions and in thoughts,
you return to the source of being.
Patient with both friends and enemies,
you accord with the way things are.
Compassionate toward yourself,
you reconcile all beings in the world.

LAO-TZU

A human being is a part of the whole that we call the universe, a part limited in time and space. He experiences himself, his thoughts and feelings, as something separated from the rest—a kind of optical illusion of his consciousness. This illusion is a prison for us, restricting us to our personal desires and to affection for only the few people nearest us. Our task must be to free ourselves from this prison by widening our circle of compassion to embrace all living beings and all of nature.

ALBERT EINSTEIN

A musician can pursue the Self while creating music, provided that he does it without selfish motivation. A teacher can pursue the Self through teaching, provided that he teaches selflessly. A businessman can pursue the Self while doing business, provided that he does it without selfish desire. A mother can pursue the Self while raising her children, provided that she does it selflessly. No matter what your field of activity, if you dedicate your work to God, it becomes a spiritual practice. If you simply do your work without personal desire for its fruits, that too is a great yoga.

SWAMI MUKTANANDA

Through love all that is bitter
    becomes sweet,
Through love all that is copper
    becomes gold.
Through love all dregs will turn
    to purest wine;
Through love all pain
    becomes medicine.
Through love the dead
    become alive,
Through love the king
    becomes a slave.

JALAL AL-DIN RUMI

On the way to God the difficulties
feel like being ground by a millstone,
like night coming at noon, like
lightning through the clouds.

But don't worry!
What must come, comes.
Face everything with love,
as your mind dissolves in God.

LALLESHWARI

The tears you shed when the ego finally loosens its clutches will never come to anyone else's attention. It happens in the privacy of your heart, in the deep stillness. This is when you drown in love. This is the cleansing bath. This is going naked before God. This is deep communion with God.

GURUMAYI CHIDVILASANANDA

A spiritual lover knows well what that voice means which says:

You, Lord God, are my whole love and desire. You are all mine, and I all Yours. Dissolve my heart into Your love so that I may know how sweet it is to serve You and how joyful it is to praise You.

THOMAS A KEMPIS

My Joy, my Hunger,
  my Shelter, my Friend,
My Food for the Journey, my Journey's End,
You are my breath, my hope,
  my companion, my craving,
  my abundant wealth.
Without You—my Life, my Love—
I would never have wandered
  across these endless countries.
You have poured out so much grace for me,
Done me so many favors,
  given me so many gifts—
I look everywhere for Your love—
Then suddenly I am filled with it.

RABI'A AL-ADAWIYA

We love God with His own love;
awareness of it deifies us.

MEISTER ECKHART

A single atom of the love of God in a heart is worth more than a hundred thousand paradises.

BAYAZID AL-BISTAMI

*Y*es, divine Love, if all souls would only be satisfied with you, what supernatural, sublime, wonderful, and inconceivable heights they would scale!

JEAN-PIERRE DE CAUSSADE

Now I will draw aside
    the veil from Love,
And in the temple
    of mine inmost soul
Behold the Friend,
    Incomparable Love.
He who would know the secret
    of both worlds
Will find the secret of them both
    is Love.

FARID AL-DIN ATTAR

There is a light that shines beyond
all things on earth, beyond us all,
beyond the heavens, beyond the
highest, the very highest heavens.
This is the light that shines in our heart.

CHANDOGYA UPANISHAD

Whenever you experience this rush of love in your heart for yourself and for everything else in this world, you should hold on to that state. That is the doorway to divinity; that is the key. Don't let go of it. The truth is that this world is full of love. This world is an embodiment of the bliss of God.

SWAMI MUKTANANDA

*B*lessed are the men and women
    who are planted on your earth,
    in your garden,
who grow as your trees and flowers grow,
    who transform their darkness to light.
Their roots plunge into darkness;
    their faces turn toward the light.
All those who love you are beautiful;
    they overflow with your presence
    so that they can do nothing but good.

ODES OF SOLOMON

Where is the door to God?
In the sound of a barking dog,
In the ring of a hammer,
In a drop of rain,
In the face of
Everyone
I see.

HAFIZ

A simple blade of grass unites
   heaven and earth
   in a split second.
A simple act of kindness ignites
   the most powerful love
   hidden in the heart.
Glory to this love. Glory to God.
Blessed are we who live by His grace.

GURUMAYI CHIDVILASANANDA

Authors and Scriptures

ABU SA'ID IBN ABI'L-KHAYR (947-1049) Persian mystic and poet known for his service to the poor.

BAYAZID AL-BISTAMI (777-848) Ecstatic Sufi saint who lived in seclusion at Bistam in Persia. He is author of many poems portraying the mystic's total absorption in God.

BROTHER LAWRENCE OF THE RESURRECTION (1614-1691) French Carmelite lay brother remembered for his continual practice of living in the awareness of God's presence.

CAUSSADE, JEAN-PIERRE DE (1675-1751) French Jesuit priest and professor. His best-known book, *Abandonment to Divine Providence*, was assembled from his letters and talks, and was published a century after his death.

CHANDOGYA UPANISHAD One of the principal Upanishads, the scriptures of India that form the basis for the philosophy of Vedanta; this work illustrates through dialogue and legend the requirements of a life of dharma, or righteous action.

CONFUCIUS (551-479 B.C.E.) Chinese philosopher who devoted his life to learning and teaching for the purpose of transforming society.

EINSTEIN, ALBERT (1879-1955) German-American physicist who developed the theory of relativity and in 1921 won the Nobel Prize in physics. Einstein advanced theories proposing entirely new ways of thinking about space, time, and gravitation.

FAKHRUDDIN ARAQI (1213-1289) Sufi Master known for entering ecstatic states during which he recited line after line of newly created, inspired poetry. His masterwork is *Lama'at* ("Divine Flashes").

FARID AL-DIN ATTAR (12th century) Prolific Sufi poet of Persia; he wrote thousands of couplets on mystical topics and several allegorical poems, including *The Conference of the Birds*.

GANDHI, MAHATMA (1869-1948) Great leader of modern India who effected lasting social reforms through the practices of nonviolence and self-restraint.

HAFIZ (1326-1390) Persian Sufi who was a court poet and professor. Originally known as Shams ud-Din Muhammad, he chose Hafiz ("memorizer") as a pen name; it designates one who knows the Qur'an by heart.

ISAAC OF NINEVEH (8th century) Syrian bishop, theologian, and solitary monk whose writings on mysticism became a fundamental source for both Eastern and Western Christians.

JALAL AL-DIN RUMI (1207-1273) Eminent Sufi poet-saint. After meeting his teacher, the ecstatic wandering saint known as Shams al-Din of Tabriz, Rumi was transformed from a sober scholar into an intoxicated singer of divine love.

KABIR (1440-1518) Poet-saint and mystic who lived as a simple weaver in Varanasi (Benares). His poems describe the universality of the Self, the greatness of the Guru, and the nature of true spirituality.

KEMPIS, THOMAS A (1379-1471) Christian theologian and monk from the Netherlands; his book *The Imitation of Christ* emphasizes spiritual rather than material life.

LALLESHWARI (14th century) Kashmiri saint who left her husband's home to devote her life to spiritual practice; her devotional poems celebrate God's omnipresence.

LAO-TZU (6th century B.C.E.) Chinese philosopher; purported author of the classic scripture of Taoism, *Tao te Ching* ("The Way and Its Power").

MAHMUD SHABISTARI (13th century) Persian sage whose writings include *The Secret Garden*, a Sufi classic.

MECHTHILD OF MAGDEBURG (13th century) German mystic and visionary who recorded her visions, ecstasies, and religious teachings in her book *Flowing Light of the Godhead*.

MEISTER ECKHART (1260-1327) German theologian and Dominican friar; author of a number of treatises charting the course of union between the individual soul and God.

NACHMAN, RABBI (1772-1810) Eminent Jewish teacher, mystic, and master of the Torah; an inspirational teacher of the Hasidic movement.

ODES OF SOLOMON (1st century) Earliest known Christian book of hymns, containing forty-two odes; the authors were probably Jewish-Christians and the originals were in Aramaic. The odes were probably chanted a cappella.

RABI'A AL-ADAWIYA (714-801) Sufi saint and mystic. She was sold into slavery as a child, but the man who bought her was so impressed by her sanctity that he set her free. She withdrew into a life of seclusion, and many disciples gathered around her.

RAMA TIRTHA, SWAMI (1873-1906) Distinguished spiritual teacher of international stature who traveled from India to introduce Vedanta in Japan and the United States in the last years of his life. He wrote many beautiful poems in the Urdu language.

SHMELKE, RABBI (1726-1778) Shmuel Shmelke Horowitz of Nikolsburg in the Eastern European country of Moravia; he was famous for his generosity to the poor.

TERESA OF AVILA, SAINT (1515-1582) Spanish Christian mystic who founded and supervised seventeen convents throughout Spain in a period of twenty years. Her books include *The Way of Perfection* and *The Interior Castle*.

THERESE OF LISIEUX, SAINT (1873-1897) French Carmelite nun whose story of her spiritual development was related in a collection of essays, *The Story of a Soul*. She defined her path to God as one of trust and absolute surrender.

TRAHERNE, THOMAS (1637-1674) Anglican clergyman and mystic whose poetry and prose meditations, *Poetical Works* and *Centuries of Meditation*, were discovered and became widely known only in the early twentieth century.

TUKARAM MAHARAJ (1608-1650) Poet-saint who was a grocer in the village of Dehu in Maharashtra, India. He wrote thousands of devotional songs describing his spiritual experiences, the realization of God, and the glory of the divine Name.

WORDSWORTH, WILLIAM (1770-1850) Central figure of the English Romantic Movement in poetry and poet laureate of England; he envisioned nature as emblematic of the mind of God.

Copyright Acknowledgments

We gratefully acknowledge the following sources:

pp. 5, 35: Stephen Mitchell, ed., *The Enlightened Mind* (New York: HarperCollins Publishers, 1991).

pp. 6, 10: A. J. Alston, trans., *Yoga and the Supreme Bliss* (London: A. J. Alston, 1982).

p. 8: Lucy Menzies, trans., *The Revelations of Mechthild of Magdeburg* (London: Longmans Green, 1953).

p. 9: Jonathan Star, ©1991. Reprinted by permission.

p. 11: Shems Friedlander, *The Whirling Dervishes* (Albany, N.Y.: State University of New York Press, 1992).

p. 13: Coleman Barks, *The Hand of Poetry* (New Lebanon, N.Y.: Omega Publishers). Reprinted by permission of the author.

pp. 15, 28: Mahatma Gandhi, *Book of Prayers* (Berkeley, Calif.: Berkeley Hills Books, 1999). Reprinted by permission of Berkeley Hills Books.

pp. 17, 31: Mitch Finley, *The Saints Speak to You Today* (Ann Arbor, Mich.: Servant Publications, 1999).

p. 18: Ch. Vaudeville, *Kabir* (London: Oxford University Press, 1974).

p. 20: Shahram Shiva and Jonathan Star, ©1990. Reprinted by permission.

p. 21: Adapted from Brother Lawrence, *The Practice of the Presence of God* (New York: Doubleday and Co., 1977).

p. 22: Adapted from Teresa of Avila, *Interior Castle* (New York: Paulist Press, 1979).

p. 23: Daniel Ladinsky, *The Subject Tonight Is Love* (North Myrtle Beach, S.C.: Pumpkin House Press, 1996). Reprinted by permission of the author.

pp. 24, 45: Margaret Smith, *Readings from the Mystics of Islam* (Westport, Conn.: PIR Publications, 1994).

p. 26: *Centuries of Meditation* (London, 1908).

p. 27: Adapted from Martin Buber, Olga Marx, trans., *Tales of the Hasidim: The Early Masters* (Schocken Books, 1975).

p. 29: Stan Padilla, *Chants and Prayers: A Native American Circle of Beauty* (Book Publishing Co.,1996).

p. 30: Moshe Mykoff, ed., *The Gentle Weapon* (Woodstock, Vt.: Jewish Lights Publishing Co., 1999).

p. 32: Adapted from Peg Streep, ed., *Confucius: The Wisdom* (Little, Brown and Co., 1995).

p. 34: Stephen Mitchell, *Tao te Ching* (New York: Harper & Row, 1988). Reprinted by permission of HarperCollins Publishers.

p. 37: Shems Friedlander, *Rumi: The Hidden Treasure* (Safina Books, 1998).

p. 38: Coleman Barks, *Lalla: Naked Song* (Athens, Ga.: Maypop Books, 1992). Reprinted by permission of the author.

p. 40: Adapted from Richard Whitford, trans., *The Imitation of Christ* (New York: Doubleday and Co., 1955).

p. 41: Charles Upton, *Doorkeeper of the Heart: Versions of Rabi'a* (Putney, Vt.: Threshold Books, 1988). Reprinted by permission of Threshold Books.

p. 44: Jean-Pierre de Caussade, *Abandonment to Divine Providence* (New York: Doubleday and Co., 1975).

p. 46: Juan Mascaro, *The Upanishads* (London: Penguin Books, 1965).

p. 49: Daniel Ladinsky, *The Gift* (New York: Penguin Putnam, 1999). Reprinted by permission of the author.

The Siddha Yoga Tradition

*S*iddha Yoga meditation is a path of spiritual unfoldment that is inspired by the grace and guidance of an enlightened Master, a Siddha Guru.

Having walked the spiritual path to its final goal, these Masters dedicate their lives to helping others complete that same journey. The journey begins with a transmission of grace known as shaktipat (*shaktipāta* in Sanskrit), an initiation by which the Siddha awakens a seeker's inner spiritual energy.

Swami Chidvilasananda, widely known as Gurumayi, is a shaktipat Guru. Since early childhood, she has been a disciple of the Siddha Master Swami Muktananda. Before his passing in 1982, he invested Swami Chidvilasananda with the full knowledge, power, and authority of the ancient tradition of Siddhas.

During the course of his lifetime, Swami Muktananda had become adept at many of the classical paths of yoga, yet he often said that his spiritual journey did not truly begin until his spiritual initiation by his own Guru. Bhagawan Nityananda, who was one of the great saints of modern India, designated Swami Muktananda as his successor before his death in 1961, directing him to give shaktipat initiation and the timeless practices of yoga to seekers everywhere. This path, which Swami Muktananda introduced to the modern world, came to be known as Siddha Yoga.

Gurumayi has carried on this tradition. Now, through the Siddha Yoga practices of meditation, chanting, mantra repetition, contemplation, and selfless service, thousands of people from diverse traditions and cultures have discovered within themselves the source of lasting happiness and peace: the experience that we are not separate from God.

Further Reading

Published by SYDA Foundation

KINDLE MY HEART
Swami Chidvilasananda

The first of Gurumayi Chidvilasananda's
books, this is an introduction to the classic
themes of the spiritual journey, arranged
thematically. There are chapters on such
subjects as meditation, mantra, control
of the senses, the Guru, the disciple,
and the state of a great being.

SMILE, SMILE, SMILE!
Poems by Gurumayi Chidvilasananda

Throughout the ages, great spiritual Masters
have offered their teachings in spontaneous
outpourings of poetry. In these poems,
Gurumayi demonstrates the mystical process
of spiritual contemplation, offering
the reader a deeper awareness of the
perfection of the soul.

(Also available on audio cassette, read by the author.)

THE MAGIC OF THE HEART:
REFLECTIONS ON DIVINE LOVE
Swami Chidvilasananda

In these profound and tender reflections on
divine love, Gurumayi Chidvilasananda makes
it clear that we must come to know our own
supreme Heart. It is here, she tells us, in the
interior of the soul, that "the Lord reveals
Himself every second of the day."

RESONATE WITH STILLNESS:
DAILY CONTEMPLATIONS
Swami Muktananda, Swami Chidvilasananda

Every sentence of this exquisite collection
of contemplations is an expression of wisdom
and love from the Siddha Masters Baba
Muktananda and Gurumayi Chidvilasananda.
The selections are arranged around twelve
themes of spiritual life, with a contemplation
for each day of the year.

REFLECTIONS OF THE SELF
Swami Muktananda

In aphoristic poetry, Baba Muktananda reflects
on the fundamental truths of spiritual life.
A mixture of wisdom, prayer, and instruction,
the book is infused with love — for the Self,
for God, for the Guru.

WHERE ARE YOU GOING?
Swami Muktananda

A comprehensive introduction to the
teachings of Siddha Yoga meditation,
this lively and anecdotal book explores
the nature of the mind, the Self, and
the inner power, as well as mantra,
meditation, and the Guru.

Other New Year's Message
Quote Books

A GOLDEN MIND, A GOLDEN LIFE

REFRESH YOUR RESOLUTION.
SMILE AT YOUR DESTINY.

WAKE UP TO YOUR INNER COURAGE
AND BECOME STEEPED IN DIVINE
CONTENTMENT

BE FILLED WITH ENTHUSIASM
AND SING GOD'S GLORY

BLAZE THE TRAIL OF EQUIPOISE

EVERYTHING HAPPENS FOR THE BEST

You can learn more about the teachings and practices
of Siddha Yoga meditation by contacting

SYDA FOUNDATION
PO BOX 600, 371 BRICKMAN RD
SOUTH FALLSBURG, NY 12779-0600, USA

TEL: (914) 434-2000

GURUDEV SIDDHA PEETH
PO GANESHPURI, PIN 401 206
DISTRICT THANA, MAHARASHTRA, INDIA

PLEASE VISIT OUR WEBSITE AT
www.siddhayoga.org

For further information on books in print by
Swami Muktananda and Gurumayi Chidvilasananda,
editions in translation, and audio and video recordings,
please contact

SIDDHA YOGA BOOKSTORE
PO BOX 600, 371 BRICKMAN RD
SOUTH FALLSBURG, NY 12779-0600, USA

TEL: (914) 434-2000 EXT. 1700

CALL TOLL-FREE FROM THE UNITED STATES
AND CANADA: 888-422-3334

FAX TOLL-FREE FROM THE UNITED STATES
AND CANADA: 888-422-3339